Book 3

Enrichment Units in Math

Written by Dianne Draze

Illustrated by Elisa Ahlin

Probability

Topology

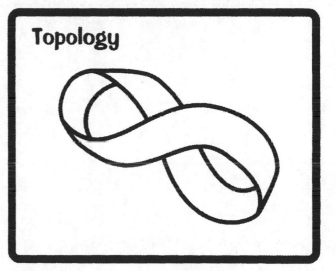

Number Characteristics

Magic Squares

Contents

First published in 2006 by Prufrock Press Inc.

Published 2021 by Routledge
605 Third Avenue, New York, NY 10017
2 Park Square, Milton Park, Abingdon, Oxon OX14 4RN

Routledge is an imprint of the Taylor & Francis Group, an informa business

ISBN 13: 978-1-5936-3070-6 (pbk)

DOI: 10.4324/9781003235033

Instructions for Teachers

Mathematics is more than simply performing computations or memorizing basic facts. It is present all around us, from the designs in granny's quilt to the patterns on our floors and walls. Mathematics is concerned with making sense of the world around us. Mathematical thinking helps us make connections, see order and think logically.

Our students should be provided with a variety of opportunities to explore mathematical ideas in ways that promote their intellectual growth and expand their views of what mathematics is. This book provides four enrichment units that involve students actively and intellectually in mathematical thinking.

Magic Squares

Magic squares have fascinated mathematicians for many years. The first one was found in China some time around 2,800 B. C. The name "magic square" probably originated in Arabia where astrologers used the arrangement of numbers to make predictions and develop horoscopes. While students have probably seen these puzzles in a variety of math books, this unit will introduce them to larger, more complicated arrays, show them techniques for making their own magic squares, and have them investigate the "magical" qualities of some classic squares. These problems require some basic computational skills, but they also require students to use inductive logic.

Topology

Topology is a field of mathematics that is like geometry in that it deals with points and lines; but unlike regular geometry, it allows objects to change shape and size. It is sometimes called rubber sheet geometry, because figures can be stretched and twisted as if they were on a rubber sheet. Topology deals with space, surface, solids, regions, and networks – those properties that are unchanged when the shape is twisted, enlarged, shrunk, or turned inside out (but not cut, torn or broken). In this fascinating unit you will find some old familiar problems like Möbius strips and the Konigsburg bridges but also some new subjects like networks and connectedness to challenge students. This unit also presents information and techniques for solving problems that are frequently presented in mathematical problem solving units. Once students have studied networks and determining the inside and outside of a shape, they will be better prepared to solve these types of problems when they encounter them in other contexts. This unit is both fun and challenging in that it presents an entirely new way to think about surfaces and shapes.

Number Characteristics

This unit encompasses a wide variety of topics as it looks at common characteristics and unusual attributes of numbers and number sequences. Students will learn about triangular numbers, square numbers, Fibonacci numbers, and prime numbers. They will be asked to analyze patterns, explain attributes, and extend sequences. While the computations are basic, the concepts are fairly sophisticated. This unit shows the real work of mathematicians, which is looking for order and relationships. Before students begin this unit they should be familiar with some basic terminology (prime, whole numbers) and operations (multiplication, addition, squaring a number).

Probability

Probability is sometimes called the mathematics of chance. It is a field of mathematics that was first formulated during the 1600s and has been used continually since by people in science and business. It is a field of mathematics that deals with predicting how likely it is that something will happen. While we typically think of probability in terms of dice throwing, it's applicable to many different activities in all areas of life where there are several possible outcomes. The emphasis on this unit is not to perform the repeated trials and statistical analysis of the trials, but to find mathematical algorithms that will allow one to predict the probability of an event happening. Before students begin this unit, they should be familiar with combinations and permutations (covered in book 2 of this math series) and be able to work with fractions and percentages with confidence.

DOI: 10.4324/9781003235033-1

3

How to Use the Units

That materials in this book may be used as extension units for the whole class or as enrichment for individuals or small groups.

While all students should have opportunities to explore mathematical ideas and go beyond practicing computational skills, for the able math students who has demonstrated mastery of concepts being taught in the classroom, enrichment options are a necessity. These units are designed to help the classroom teacher provide for these needs. They lend themselves easily to a math center arrangement with each student having an individual folder and a checklist to record progress. Some of the units can also be used as extensions for units the whole class is studying.

Providing enrichment options need not be burdensome to the teacher. While the teacher may want to check some of the work himself/herself, it is not necessary for everything to be checked by the teacher as it is completed. Work can be checked by another student or self-corrected. Keys can be provided for students who are to check each other's or their own answers.

Remember, the emphasis for enrichment units is not "How many right?" or "How quickly did you finish?" The emphasis should be on promoting thinking, developing perseverance, expanding students' views of mathematics, enjoying a challenge, and on keeping able math students actively involved and enthused about math.

Materials

Magic Squares
- paper
- pencil
- calculator (optional)

Topology
- pencil
- paper
- scissors
- tape
- colored pencils

Number Characteristics
- pencil
- paper

Probability
- pencil
- paper
- coins
- dice (optional)
- deck of cards (optional)
- spinner (optional)

Independent Study Contract

Name_____

I began this unit on _____ on _____
date

Work Record

Date	I worked on	✓ when completed

Conditions of working independently_____

_____

_____

_____

_____

_____

_____   _____
teacher's signature   student's signature

Name _____

Magic squares have fascinated mathematicians for many years. The first one was found on a scroll called Loh-Shu that was created in China some time around 2,800 B.C. From China, the magic squares spread to India, Japan, the Middle East, Africa and finally to Europe and America. The name "magic square" probably originated in Arabia where astrologers used the arrangement of numbers to make predictions and develop horoscopes. Wise men in several countries called the construction of these arrays a secret science and used them for fortune telling and to ward off bad luck. In the Middle Ages, magic squares were even considered a protection against the Plague. Even today magic squares are imprinted on pieces of metal and worn as talismans by certain groups in India.

A **magic square** is an array of numbers that is arranged in the following way:
- There are the same number of rows and columns.
- No number is used more than once.
- The sum of every row, column and each of the two diagonals is the same number, the number said to be the **magic sum** or the **magic constant**.
- While the basic magic squares are formed using consecutive numbers beginning with the number 1, squares can be adapted by changing the order of the numbers, by adding a constant to all numbers, or by using multiples of the basic number sequence.

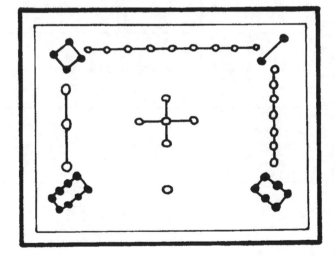

On the right is the first magic square. It is a 3-by-3 square. The numbers are represented by white and black dots. The numbers represented by white dots were considered heavenly numbers. The numbers represented by black dots were considered earthly numbers.

Translate the numbers from the Loh-Shu magic square into our number system and record the numbers in the grid on the right. Add the numbers in each row, column and diagonal to find the magic sum.

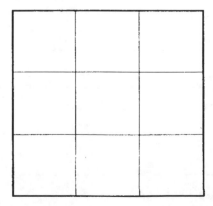

The magic sum for the Loh-Shu square is _____

 DOI: 10.4324/9781003235033-3

Name_____

Here are two magic squares that have been begun for you. Complete each one by placing the numbers 1 through 9 in the squares so that the sum of the rows and columns is 15.

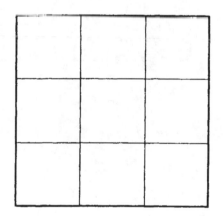

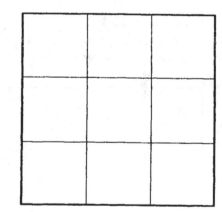

There are many different ways that the numbers 1 through 9 can be arranged in a 3 x 3 square that will give a magic sum of 15. Find three other arrangements and write them on these grids.

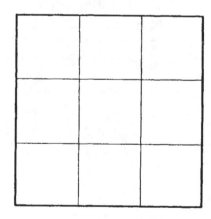

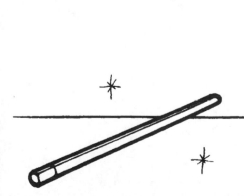

Name _____

1. Arrange the numbers 3, 6, 9, 12, 15, 18, 21, 24, and 27 in the squares so that the sums of all the rows, columns and diagonals are 45.

18		
	12	

3. Arrange the numbers 4, 5, 6, 7, 8, 9, 11, and 12 in the squares so that the sums of all the rows, columns and diagonals are 24.

	8	

5. Arrange the numbers 2, 6, 10, 14, 18, 22, 26, 30, and 34 in the squares so that the sums of all the rows, columns and diagonals are 54.

2. Arrange the numbers 4, 8, 12, 16, 20, 24, 28, 32, and 36 in the squares so that the sums of all the rows, columns, and diagonals are 60.

8		
16		

4. Arrange the numbers 2, 4, 6, 8, 10, 12, 14, 16, and 18 in the squares so that the sums of all the rows, columns and diagonals are 30.

Name_____

Here is a 4-by-4 magic square that has been started for you. Place the numbers 1 through 16 in this magic square so that the rows, columns and diagonals add up to 34. Make one other arrangement of the same numbers in the square on the right that will give the same sum.

7		1	
	13	8	
	3		5
9		15	

Here is a 5-by-5 magic square that uses the numbers 1 through 25. Complete the square and give the magic sum.

		19	2	15
10	18			22
	5	13	21	
4			8	16
11	24	7	20	3

The magic sum is _____

Name _____

Because magic squares were thought to have magical powers and the people who created them were special, mathematicians who created the magic squares used many tricks (like purposely putting mistakes in them) so ordinary people would not discover their secrets. Here are several arrays of numbers. Some of them are magic and some are not. Find the magic sum for each array and find which ones are magic. Mark out the ones that are not magic.

4	9	2
3	5	7
8	1	6

A

6	11	5
10	2	8
5	7	9

B

8	2	11
10	7	4
3	12	6

C

16	2	3	13
5	11	10	8
9	7	6	12
4	14	15	1

D

19	25	1	7	13
24	5	6	12	18
4	10	11	17	23
9	15	16	22	3
14	20	21	2	8

E

6
4 3

Name_____

An arithmetic progression is a sequence of numbers that are related in such a way that each number is the sum of the preceding number plus some constant number. Here are some examples:

3, 5, 7, 9, 11   Rule: add 2
4, 14, 24, 34   Rule: add 10
1, 5, 9, 13, 17   Rule: add 4

If you look closely at the rows and columns of the magic square you will find that several of the numbers form arithmetic progressions. In this magic square the progressions are 1, 5, 9 (add 4) and 3, 5, 7 (add 2) . There are two other progressions (2, 5, 8 and 4, 5, 6). Find them and circle them.

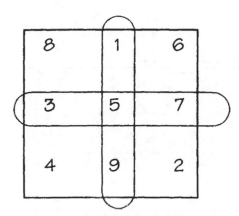

Mark and list the four progressions in these magic squares.

8	18	4
6	10	14
16	2	12

18	3	24
21	15	9
6	27	12

13	6	11
8	10	12
9	14	7

1. _____

_____

_____

_____

2. _____

_____

_____

_____

3. _____

_____

_____

_____

Name _____

There are several procedures for constructing magic squares. The following is a common procedure for constructing magic square with an odd number of cells (9, 25, 49, etc.). Here are the instructions for a square of 9 cells, but the same procedure will work for larger odd-celled squares.

1. You may begin with any number, but for this demonstration, we will use the number 1.

2. Draw a nine-cell square and write the number 1 in the center top cell.

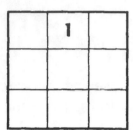

3. Each consecutive number will be placed in a cell that is one cell to the right and one cell above the previous number. When this movement would place the number outside the square (as it would with the number 2), the number is placed in a cell that is in the same row or column, but is on the bottom row or the left column. The number 2, then, goes in the right-hand cell on the bottom row. Since the number 3 would be outside the square, it is placed in the left column in the center row.

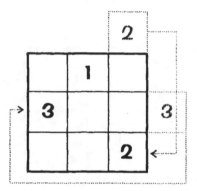

4. When a number cannot be placed in a cell because that cell is already occupied, it is placed directly below the previous number. The number 4 is placed below 3.

5. 5 and 6 are easily placed using the diagonal rule.

6. 7 cannot be placed in the diagonal position, because it would fall outside of the square for both a row or column position. In this case, it is treated as if the cell is occupied by another number, and it is placed below the 6.

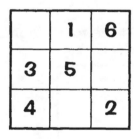

7. 8 and 9 can be placed following the rules for numbers that when placed diagonally fall outside of the square.

The sums of all the rows, columns and diagonals of this magic square are _____.

Name _____

Follow the rules for placing numbers in a magic square with an odd number of cells to make a nine-celled magic square that starts with the number 3 and another one that starts with 12.

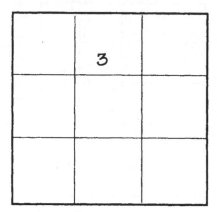

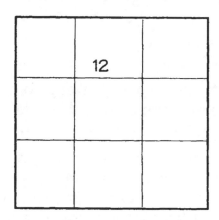

The magic sum is _____.

The magic sum is _____.

Use the rules for placing numbers in a magic square with an odd number of cells to make a 25-celled magic square that starts with the number 1. The first four numbers have been placed for you.

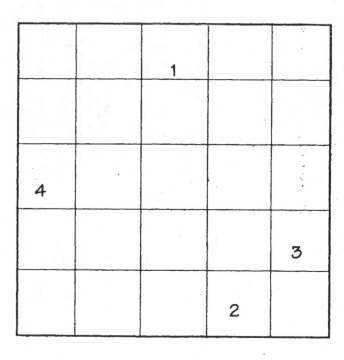

The magic sum is _____.

© Taylor & Francis —Enrichment Units in Math

Name _____

There are standard procedures for placing numbers in even-cell magic squares that are multiples of four (like 16 cells). Here is the procedure for a 16-cell square.

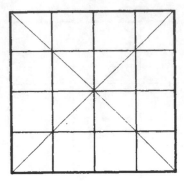

1. After drawing the 16-cell square, diagonals are drawn.

2. Start with the number 1 (though other numbers may also be used when you create your own squares).

3. You are going to fill in each number consecutively beginning in the upper left corner and working across the row to the right. Whenever you come to a square that has the diagonal drawn on it, you will skip that square and that number. The first number you will write, therefore, is the number 2 in the second cell.

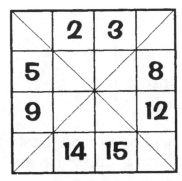

4. The number 3 is written in the next cell but the number 4 is skipped. Continue writing numbers in the blank squares, skipping numbers where the cell has a line through it.

5. Erase the diagonals and fill in the remaining blank cells with the unused numbers. But this time you will start with the highest number (in this case 16). Write 16 in the top left cell, 13 in the top right cell, and so forth, filling in the missing numbers (11, 10, 7, 6, 4 and 1).

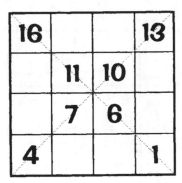

What is the magic sum for this square? _____

16	2	3	13
5	11	10	8
9	7	6	12
4	14	15	1

Name_____

Follow the rules for placing numbers in a magic square with an even number of cells to make a 16-celled magic square that starts with the number 4.

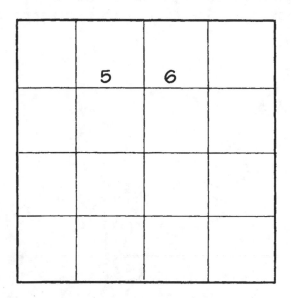

The magic sum for this magic square is _____.

These two 16-cell magic squares have been started for you. Continue placing numbers

The magic sum is _____

The magic sum is _____

Name _____

One of the more famous magic squares was made by a German artist named Albrecht Dürer and was included in one of his paintings called "Melancholia." The painting was created in 1514. The magic square used the numbers 1 through 16 in a magic square that had many special properties. This is what his magic square looked like. See if you can discover some of the special properties.

16	3	2	13
5	10	11	8
9	6	7	12
4	15	14	1

1. The year the painting was made is in the square. Circle it.

2. What is the sum of all the rows, columns and diagonals?_____

3. What is the sum of the four numbers in the smaller 2x2 corner squares?_____

4. Adjacent numbers are numbers that are next to each other, like 16 and 3. In each row, the sum of one pair of adjacent numbers is _____ and the sum of the other adjacent numbers is _____.

5. In each column, the sum of one pair of adjacent numbers is _____ and the sum of the other adjacent numbers is _____.

6. The sum of the two center numbers in the top row (3 and 2) and the two center numbers in the bottom row is _____.

7. The sum of the two center numbers in the column on the left (5 and 9) and the two center numbers of the column on the right is _____.

Looking for Properties

Name_____

Here is another large magic square that has many special features. Study the square and see how many special relationships you can discover.

1	59	56	14	2	60	53	15
46	24	27	33	47	21	28	34
32	38	41	19	31	37	44	18
51	9	6	64	50	12	5	63
3	57	54	16	4	58	55	13
48	22	25	35	45	23	26	36
30	40	43	17	29	39	42	20
49	11	8	62	52	10	7	61

1. The magic sum of the large magic square is _____.

2. Each quarter is a _____ x _____ magic square.

3. The magic sum of the four smaller magic squares is _____.

4. The sum of the four numbers in each 2x2 square is _____.

5. Each quarter contains four overlapping 3x3 squares. The sum of the corners of each 3x3 square is _____.

6. Find the four 5x5 squares in the larger 8x8 square.

   a. The corner numbers of the top left square are _____, _____, _____, _____.

   b. The corner numbers of the top right square are _____, _____, _____, _____.

   c. The corner numbers of the bottom left square are _____, _____, _____, _____.

   d. The corner numbers of the bottom right square are _____, _____, _____, _____.

Name _____

Here are some magic squares that have some of the numbers missing. Fill in numbers that will correctly complete the magic squares and find the magic sum for each square.

9	2	
	6	8
	10	

1. magic sum = _____

		34
36	28	20
	32	

2. magic sum = _____

40		20
	25	
30		

3. magic sum = _____

13	37	61
31		

4. magic sum = _____

14	10	
	18	2
	26	

5. magic sum = _____

45		9
69	15	33

6. magic sum = _____

Completing Magic Squares

Name_____

Here are some magic squares that have some of the numbers missing. Fill in numbers that will correctly complete the magic squares and find the magic sum for each square.

16	3		5
1	12	7	
	13	2	11
9			4

1. magic sum = _____

8	5.5		
	3	8.5	5
7.5	6	1.5	
	4.5	7	6.5

2. magic sum = _____

23	12			9
4		7	21	15
10		13		16
	5	19	8	
17	6		14	3

3. magic sum = _____

8	1	1 1/2	6 1/2
2 1/2		5	4
	3 1/2	3	
2		7 1/2	1/2

4. magic sum = _____

Name _____

These magic squares are bordered squares. When each square layer is removed, the remaining square is still a magic square. Study the magic squares and then answer the questions.

2	23	25	7	8
4	16	9	14	22
21	11	13	15	5
20	12	17	10	6
18	3	1	19	24

1. The magic sum for the 5x5 square is _____

2. The magic sum for the 3x3 square is _____

18	27	26	61	62	65	28
59	30	35	51	53	36	23
58	32	38	45	40	50	24
57	49	43	41	39	33	25
22	48	42	37	44	34	60
19	46	47	31	29	52	63
54	55	56	21	20	17	64

3. The magic sum for the 3x3 square is _____.

4. The magic sum for the 5x5 square is _____.

5. The magic sum for the 7x7 square is _____.

© Taylor & Francis —Enrichment Units in Math

Name_____

Topology was originated by a Swiss mathematician named Leonard Euler (pronounced Oiler) in the 1700s. It is a field of mathematics that is like geometry in that it deals with points and lines; but unlike regular geometry, it allows objects to change shape and size. It is sometimes called rubber sheet geometry, because figures can be stretched and twisted as if they were on a rubber sheet. Measurement of length, width, height, volume or angles has no place in topology. Topology looks at other important properties of figures. It deals with space, surface, regions, and networks – those properties that are unchanged when the shape is twisted, enlarged, shrunk, or turned inside out (but not cut, torn or broken).

In topology a straight line is just the same as a wavy line.

   is the same as

A sphere is equivalent to a cube, and a cube is equivalent to an apple.

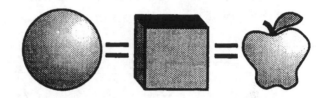

Topologically equivalent shapes can be twisted and stretched into the same shape without connecting or disconnecting any points on the surface of the figure.

 is equivalent to which is equivalent to

Imagine that the following numerals and letters are made of a piece of clay. You can see that you can mold and rotate each one (without breaking the clay or adding any new pieces of clay) to make to the other ones. These numerals and letters are topologically equivalent.

1   2   ᘔ   3   L   M   S

---

1. Circle the numerals and letters below that are equivalent to the numerals above; that is, they could be pulled or twisted (but not joined together or cut) to make a shape that is like the shapes above.

        4   5   6   7   8   9   A   B

        C   D   E   F   G   H   I   J

© Taylor & Francis —*Enrichment Units in Math*   DOI: 10.4324/9781003235033-4   **21**

Name _____

In regular geometry, two regular polygons are equivalent if their line segments are equal and their angles are equal. Triangles A and B and equivalent. Triangle C is not equivalent to either Triangle A or B because its angles and sides are not equal to those of A or B.

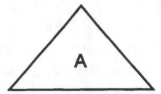 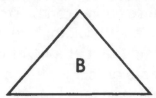 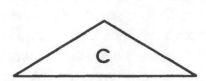

When you look at two figures in topology and try to decide if they are equivalent, it helps if you can picture the figures as being drawn on a rubber sheet that can be stretched but cannot be torn. In topology all three figures below are equivalent because:
- the order of the points on the figures is the same for all three figures
- the point inside the figure is the same for all three figures.

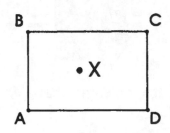 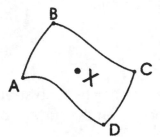 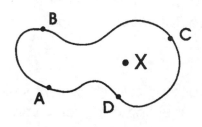

Match each figure on the right with an equivalent figure on the left.

_____ 1.    A.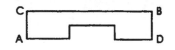

_____ 2. 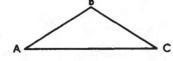   B.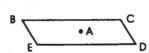

_____ 3.   C.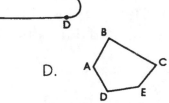

_____ 4. 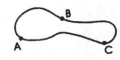   D.

_____ 5. 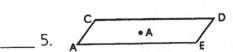   E.

Name_____

Topology is known as the mathematics of distortion. In the field of topology, any closed curve that divides the plane into one inside and one outside is equivalent to a circle. Therefore a triangle, a square, and an irregular polygon are equivalent to a circle. They all have one inside and one outside. They are what we call simple closed curves.

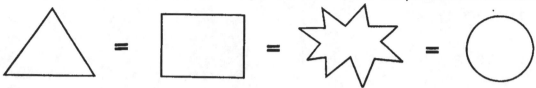

The figures below are not equivalent to a circle because they divide the plane into more than one inside and one outside.

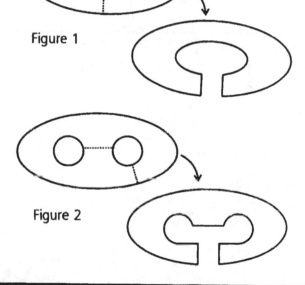

If you cut figure 1 in one place, you would have a figure that is equivalent to a circle. That is, if it were made of clay, it could be stretched into that shape. If two shapes can be made equivalent with one cut, they are said to be **singly connected.**

Figure 1

Figure 2 could be cut in two places in such a way that it would be equivalent to a circle. If something needs two cuts to make it equivalent, it is said to be **doubly-connected.** Once it is cut, it could be stretched into a circular shape.

Figure 2

Put a **=** next to the shapes if they are equivalent to a circle, a **1** if they are singly-connected, a **2** if they are doubly-connected.

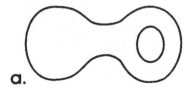

a.

b.

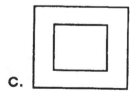

c.

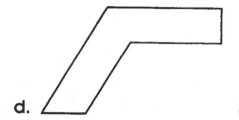

d.

e.

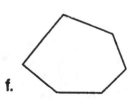

f.

Three-Dimensional Equivalence

Name _____

The idea of equivalence in two dimensions is also applicable to three-dimensional objects. Just as every simple closed figure is topologically equivalent to a circle, every solid three-dimensional figure with no holes is equivalent to a sphere. That is, if a sphere were made of clay, it could be molded into a variety of shapes as long as it were not torn or other pieces of clay were not added to it.

A cube, cone and sphere are topologically equivalent.

A torus (doughnut-shaped object) with one hole in it would be equivalent to other objects that have one hole in them.

Likewise, a shape with two holes in it would be equivalent to other solids with two holes in them.

Write a 1, 2 or 3 next to these objects according to whether they are equivalent to a sphere **(1)**, a doughnut **(2)** or a disk with two holes **(3)**.

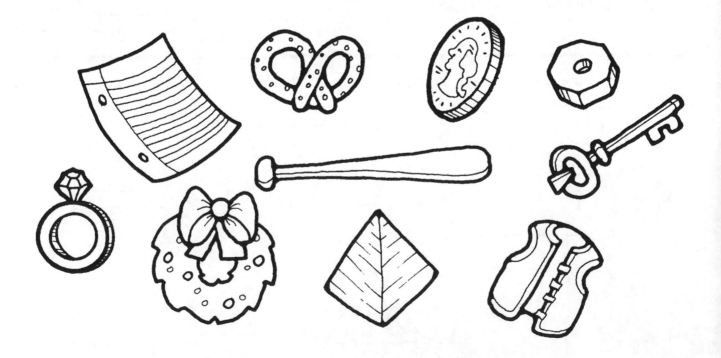

Name_____

One idea that is used in several areas of topology is the concept of the simple closed curve and whether points lie inside or outside the curve. A nineteenth century French mathematician named Jordan gave us the following rule about figures:

> A **simple closed curve** is a two-dimensional figure that divides the plane into two regions – an inside and an outside.

A circle is a simple closed curve that has one inside and one outside.

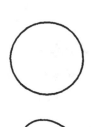

A figure 8 has two insides and one outside, so it is not a simple closed curve.

The letter E has one outside and no inside, so it is not a simple closed curve.

E

The doughnut-shaped drawing has two outsides and one inside, so it is not a simple closed curve.

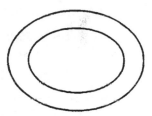

These are simple closed curves.

These are not simple closed curves.

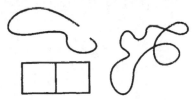

Circle the figures in this group that are simple closed curves.

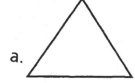

a.

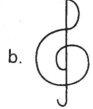

b.

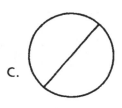

c.

d.

e.

f.

Name _____

In order to accurately apply Jordan's rule for determining simple closed curves, you must be able to determine where the inside and outside of a shape is. In the figures you just looked at, it was easy to determine what was the inside and what was the outside. Some figures are very complicated and you need some systematic way to tell what is the inside and what is the outside. In this example, it is easy to see that the letter X is inside the curve and the letter Y is outside the curve.

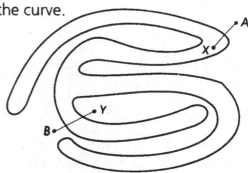

Inside-Outside Test

In complicated figures, you can tell whether a point is inside or outside a curve by drawing a line from the point to some point outside the figure and counting the number of lines it crosses.

- If it crosses an **odd** number of lines, it is **inside** the curve.
- If it crosses and **even** number of lines, it is **outside** the curve.

Line $\overline{XA}$ crosses one line, so X is inside the curve.
Line $\overline{YB}$ crosses two lines, so it is outside the curve.

Tell whether the points in these drawings are inside or outside the figures.

A _____   B _____   C _____   D _____

E _____   F _____   G _____   H _____

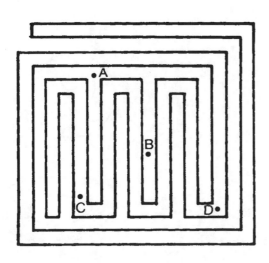

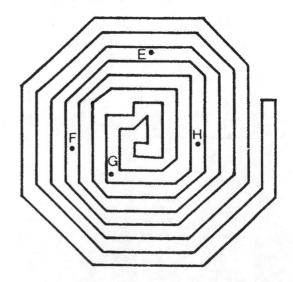

© Taylor & Francis —**Enrichment Units in Math**

Name_____

A problem that you may be asked to solve at some point in your schooling states, *"There are three houses, A, B and C, that need to be connected to water, gas and electricity (X, Y and Z), but the lines connecting the utilities cannot cross each other."* Here is a technique for solving this problem.

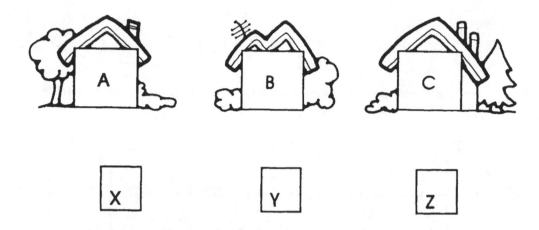

1. Draw lines connecting houses A and B to the three utilities.

2. Before attempting to connect house C, determine whether C is inside or outside the closed curve formed by the outer most lines connecting A and B to the utilities.

3. Decide whether each of the utilities (X, Y and Z) are inside or outside this closed curve.

4. Is it possible to draw a line from C to X, Y and Z without crossing the lines connecting A and B to X, Y and Z? **(possible, impossible)**

5. Try this same problem with only two houses and two utilities.

6. Try to connect two houses and four utilities.

Euler's Theorem

Name _____

Relationship Between Regions, Corners and Arcs

To discover one of Euler's theorems, you need to carefully examine several figures. When you look at each figure, you will be counting the number of regions (insides and outsides) the figure divides the plane into, the number of vertices (points were lines meet) and arcs (straight or curved lines).

This figure has 3 regions, 3 arcs and 2 vertices.

Here are 6 figures. Count the regions, vertices and arcs in each figure and record the information on the chart.

1. 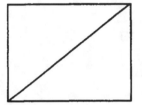 2.  3.  4.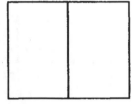

	regions	vertices	arcs
1.			
2.			
3.			
4.			
5.			
6.			

5.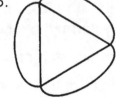

6.

Euler's Theorem states that if R = regions, V = vertices, and A = arcs, then

R + V = A + 2

7. Did this rule hold true for all the figures above? _____

8. On the back of this paper draw two other figures and verify that the rule is true for these two figures.

Name _____

This is an area of topology that has modern day applications in the field of advanced circuit design, but it began hundreds of years ago because a town in Germany with a river that ran through the center of the town had seven bridges connecting the various parts of the city. During their spare time the people liked to walk the route that took them over the bridges. They wondered if it was possible to follow a path that led to all parts of the city and crossed each bridge only once. When they were unable to solve this problem on their own, they asked Euler to solve the problem for them.

Euler wanted to not only solve this problem but also to state a general rule that would apply to all such problems. He began by drawing a diagram that showed the parts of the city as points and the bridges connecting the different parts as lines. He called the drawing a **network**. His network looked like this:

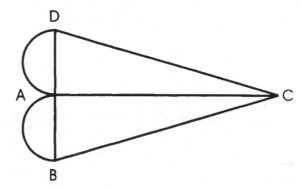

Euler called a network **closed** if:
- the path over the network began and ended at the same point.
- the path touched each point (or vertex)
- the path passed over each line segment only once.

A network was **open** if:
- the path over the network touched each point
- the path passed over each line segment only once
- the path ended at some point that was different from the starting point.

___

Try to trace over each each of these networks without retracing any line or lifting your pencil. Put a **C** if it is possible to trace it and return to the starting point, an **O** if it is possible to trace it but not to return to the starting point, and **NT** if the path is not traceable.

1.

2.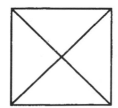

3.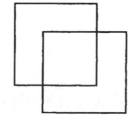

4.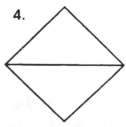

Name _____

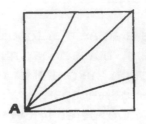

After Euler drew a network, he looked at the number of arcs (straight or curved lines) that met at a point (vertex). Each vertex was then described as either even or odd according to the number of arcs forming the vertex. In this network there are 5 arcs that intersect at vertex A, so it is odd.

1. Tell whether each vertex in these drawings is odd or even.

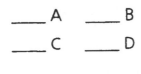

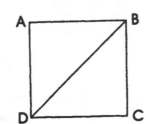

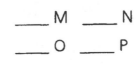

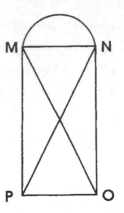

Euler's Theorem

After examining several networks, Euler formulated a rule (theorem) that would allow people to determine whether a network was traceable or not. It said:

- *If every point is even, the network is closed and can be traced so that the path will go through all points and will go over each line segment only once.*

- *If there are two odd points and all the rest are even, then the path is open and can be traced but the path will not return to the starting point.*

2. Count the number of lines intersecting at each vertex. Tell how many even and odd vertices each network has and whether the figure is closed (**C**), open (**O**), or not traceable (**NT**). For networks that are traceable, trace a path.

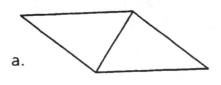

a.

b.

c.

_____   _____   _____

3. Look back at the network for the Konigsburg bridges (lesson 9). Is this network closed, open, or not traceable? _____

Name_____

The game of Sprouts is related to the field of networks that was originated by Euler. In this game two people create networks by drawing lines and points. Here are the rules for playing this game.

1. Mark two points on a piece of paper.

2. One player draws an arc from one point to another point or from one point back to itself and then adds an additional point on the arc.

3. The players take turns drawing line segments. When they draw a line they have to add a point on the line they drew.

4. Each line must join two points or must form a loop with one point.

5. No line can cross itself, cross another line, or pass through a point.

6. No more than three arcs can start or finish at a point. In the case of a loop that begins and ends at the point, each end of the loop is counted as an arc.

7. The last person who is able to play is the winner.

Play the game with a partner.

Brussel Sprouts is a variation of this game that begins with three or more points instead of just two. After you have mastered Sprouts, try Brussel Sprouts.

Name _____

Everyone knows that a piece of paper has two sides. Right? Well not in topology. A German mathematician named Augustus Möbius worked with a concept in topology that allowed a piece of paper to have only one side. It is now called a **Möbius strip**. While it seems like a frivolous plaything, manufacturers of conveyor belts, recording tape and electronic resistors have all found uses for this concept.

Investigation:

1. Make a strip of paper and tape it in such a way that it forms a circle. Mark a point A on one side. Then begin at point A and draw a line the length of the strip. When you return back to point A you will have drawn a line on only one side of the paper.

2. Next take a similar strip of paper and make a circle but put a half twist (180°) in it before you tape it. This is a Möbius strip. As before, mark point A and begin drawing a line along the strip. When you return back to point A you will see that you have made a mark on both sides of the strip without ever turning it over or lifting your pencil. Your strip has only one side.

3. Make three other strips, putting 2 half twists, 3 half twists (1 1/2 full twists) and 4 half twists (2 full twists) in them and tape them together. Then draw a line down the center of each strip without lifting your pencil until you return to your starting point. Describe the results below.

twists	results	one-sided or two-sided?
0		
1/2		
1		
1 1/2		
2		

© Taylor & Francis —**Enrichment Units in Math**

Cutting Möbius Strips

Name_____

In this investigation you will be discovering what happens when you make Möbius strips with different number of twists and you cut a them in different ways (down the middle, one-quarter of the way from the edge, or one-third the way from the edge).

Cut 10 pieces of paper that are 11 inches long and about 1 inch wide. The instructions in the chart will tell you how many twists you are to put in your strip before you tape it together. After you tape the strip, cut the strip according to the directions in the chart. Describe the results.

half twists	location of cut	describe the results
0	1/2	
1	1/2	
1	1/3	
1	1/4	
2	1/2	
2	1/3	
3	1/2	
3	1/3	
3	1/4	

What general statements can you make to describe the results you could expect from cutting a Möbius strip with any given number of twists?_____

_____

_____

Four Color Map

Name _____

Augustus Möbius was a teacher and gave his students this question, *"How many colors are needed to color any flat map in such a way that no two areas with a common border are the same color?"* Not only were his students stumped by this question, but mathematicians have pondered this question for a long time. For many years, mathematicians knew that four colors seemed to be sufficient to color any map. They could not devise a map that needed five colors, but they thought that perhaps there might be such a map. Finally in 1976, after an enormous number of computer calculations, it was proved that **no more that four colors are ever needed to color a map so that adjacent areas are not the same color**. This rule only applies to two-dimensional maps, however. It is possible to create a map on a torus (doughnut shape) that needs as many as seven colors and a Möbius strip requires six colors.

---

1. What is the least number of colors required for coloring each of the following figures so that no two regions sharing a border are the same color? After you determine the number of colors, color each map.

a.    b. 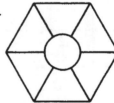   c.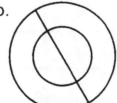

d. 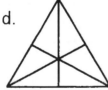   e. 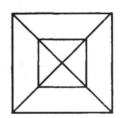   f.

2. Make a map that requires four colors. Give this map to a friend and ask him or her to color it.

Name_____

While most people probably think that mathematicians spend all their time adding, subtracting, multiplying and dividing, this is not what mathematicians do at all. For hundreds of years mathematicians have been interested in different characteristics of shapes and numbers. They have spent their time studying how numbers relate to one another and how they can be used to describe the real world. They have sought rules that would be true of all things with common characteristics; for instance, all squares, all circumferences, or all even numbers. Mathematicians have inquiring, creative minds. They look at each problem as a puzzle to be solved. They are delighted when they find a new relationship between numbers or between numbers and the real world.

A mathematician would look at a string of numbers like the one below and ask, "Are these numbers related in any way?" Look for the way the numbers are related and fill in the missing numbers in the sequence.

1   3   6   10   15   ____   ____   ____   45

---

1. How would you describe the relationship between the numbers shown above? _____
_____

2. Look at the following sequences of numbers and write a rule that describes the relationship between the numbers.

a. 1, 3, 5, 7, 9, 11, 13, 15 _____

b. 1, 4, 7, 10, 13, 16, 19, 22 _____

c. 1, 2, 4, 8, 16, 32, 64 _____

d. 1, 4, 9, 16, 25, 36, 49 _____

e. 10, 20, 30, 40, 50, 60, 70 _____

f. 200, 100, 50, 25, 12.5, 6.25 _____

Name _____

Below are the first five **triangular numbers**. They are called triangular numbers because they can be expressed graphically with triangular arrangements. Each triangle has a base that is one unit more than the base of the preceding triangle. The sum of the units in each triangle is the triangular number.

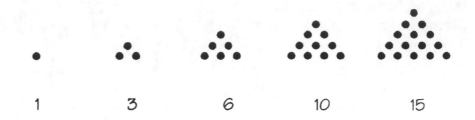

| 1 | 3 | 6 | 10 | 15 |

This chart shows the next triangular numbers that are not shown above. Complete the chart. Draw the 13th and 14th triangular numbers in the space on the right.

position	number
6th	21
7th	28
8th	36
9th	_____
10th	_____
11th	_____
12th	_____
13th	_____
14th	_____

Name_____

Square numbers are numbers that can be shown graphically by a square configuration. Each representation has the same number of units horizontally as vertically. Here are the first four square numbers.

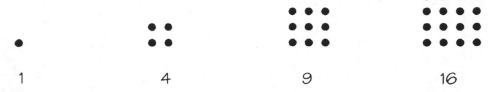

1. Each square number can be written as a product of a number and itself. Finish this chart to show the next six square numbers.

    1 = 1 x 1   36 = _____

    4 = 2 x 2   49 = _____

    9 = 3 x 3   64 = _____

    16 = 4 x 4   _____

    25 = _____ x _____   _____

2. What rule can you state for finding the nth square number?_____

3. Square numbers can also be written as a sum of numbers. Finish the sequence of square numbers, writing each one as a sum in the same pattern that is shown.

    4 = 1 + 3

    9 = 1 + 3 + _____

    16 = 1 + 3 + _____ + _____

    25 = _____ + _____ + _____ + _____ + _____

    _____

    _____

    _____

    _____

Name _____

1. Complete this chart to show the first 10 triangular numbers and first 10 square numbers.

position	triangular	square
1st		
2nd		
3rd		
4th		
5th		
6th		
7th		
8th		
9th		
10th		

2. Square numbers can be represented as a sum of consecutive triangular numbers. Check your chart and then finish these sums.

1 = 1

4 = 1 + 3

9 = 3 + 6

16 = _____

25 = _____

_____

_____

_____

_____

Name_____

Like square numbers, **rectangular numbers** can be shown graphically in a rectangular array. The rectangles are made so that each number has one more row and one more column than the preceding number. Here are the first four rectangular numbers.

$$2 = 1 \times 2 \qquad 6 = 2 \times 3 \qquad 12 = 3 \times 4 \qquad 20 = 4 \times 5$$

1. Write a multiplication problem to show the next four rectangular numbers.

_____   _____

_____   _____

2. Rectangular numbers also have the characteristic that they can be written as the sum of even numbers beginning with 2. Here are the first three rectangular numbers. Write addition facts for the next six rectangular numbers.

$$2 = 2 \qquad\qquad 6 = 2 + 4 \qquad\qquad 12 = 2 + 4 + 6$$

_____   _____   _____

_____   _____   _____

3. Another interesting characteristic of rectangular numbers is that they are twice the corresponding triangular numbers. Complete this chart for the first 10 rectangular numbers and the corresponding triangular number.

rectangular	triangular		rectangular	triangular
2	1		_____	_____
6	3		_____	_____
12	6		_____	_____
_____	_____		_____	_____
_____	_____		_____	_____

Name _____

When early mathematicians began looking at numbers, they discovered that most numbers could be written as the product of two numbers. For instance 6 = 2 x 3 and 48 = 6 x 8. They found some numbers, though, that could only be written as a product of 1 and the number. These numbers they called **prime numbers**. Prime numbers are any number greater than 1 that can only be expressed as a product of 1 and itself. The first five prime numbers are 2, 3, 5, 7, and 11.

1. Circle all the prime numbers on this chart of numbers.

1	2	3	4	5	6	7	8	9	10
11	12	13	14	15	16	17	18	19	20
21	22	23	24	25	26	27	28	29	30
31	32	33	34	35	36	37	38	39	40
41	42	43	44	45	46	47	48	49	50
51	52	53	54	55	56	57	58	59	60
61	62	63	64	65	66	67	68	69	70
71	72	73	74	75	76	77	78	79	80
81	82	83	84	85	86	87	88	89	90
91	92	93	94	95	96	97	98	99	100

Prime Pairs

2. Prime pairs are two prime numbers that differ by 2. Here are the first two prime pairs between one and 100. Write the rest of them.

(3, 5)   (5, 7) _____ _____ _____ _____ _____ _____

Goldbach's Conjecture

Name_____

A mathematician named Goldbach made the following discovery about the relationship between even numbers and prime numbers. While he found that this relationship was true for every even number he tried, he could not prove it was true for all even numbers. Since there are an infinite number of even numbers, he could not try every number. Since it could not be proved, it is called a conjecture.

Goldbach's Conjecture
Every even number greater than 2 can be expressed as the sum of two prime numbers.

1. Here are the sums for the first six numbers. Refer to your prime number chart from lesson 6 and write sums for the remaining numbers. If there is more than one way to express the number, write it as many ways as possible.

4 = 2 + 2

6 = 3 + 3

8 = 3 + 5

10 = 5 + 5 or 7 + 3

12 = 7 + 5

14 = 7 + 7 or 3 + 11

16 = _____

18 = _____

20 = _____

22 = _____

28 = _____

34 = _____

46 = _____

52 = _____

68 = _____

70 = _____

88 = _____

96 = _____

100 = _____

106 = _____

Name _____

Use your prime number chart (lesson 6) to help you solve these problems.

1. Alfred has between 50 and 60 pieces of candy to share with his group of friends. If he divides it between himself and two of his friends (three people total), he has 2 pieces left over. If he divides it between himself and four of his friends, he has 4 pieces left over. How many pieces of candy does he have?

2. What is the largest number less than 500 that is the product of exactly two prime numbers?

3. What is the smallest odd number you can find that is the sum of three different prime numbers?

Name_____

When you are using words, palindromes are words or phrases that read the same backwards and forward. Some common palindromes are:

tut tut

Madam, I am Adam.

Rise to vote sir.

Was it a bar or a bat I saw?

Palindromes can also be numbers that read the same backwards and forwards. They are numbers like **23432** or **565**.

The interesting thing about numerical palindromes is that if you take any two-digit (or greater) number and add the digits of the number to the digits in reverse order and continue this process with each successive sum, you will eventually get a numerical palindrome. Here are three examples.

67	512	352
+ 76	+ 215	+ 253
143	727	605
+ 341		+ 506
484		1111

Try this process with three other numbers, adding the numbers and their reversals until you get a palindrome.

Name _____

Thousands of years ago the people of Babylon used a rope with knots in it to form a right angle so that they could measure plots of land after the rainy season each year. Knots were tied at intervals of 3 units, 7 units and 12 units. By holding the rope so that one side was 3 units long, one was 4 units long and one was 5 units long, they were able to consistently form a right angle.

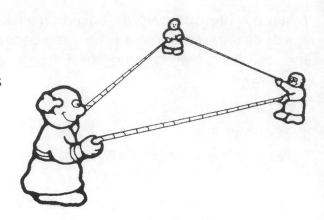

Hundreds of years later the Greek mathematician Pythagoras used this information to formulate the Pythagorean theorem. This theorem says:

if a, b, and c are the sides of a triangle, then for any right triangle, $a^2 + b^2 = c^2$.

With the numbers the Babylonians used you can see that $3^2 + 4^2 = 5^2$ or $9 + 16 = 25$.

---

1. Complete this chart for other Pythagorean triples.

	a	b	c	$a^2 + b^2 = c^2$
a.	5	12	13	_____
b.	7	24	25	_____
c.	9	40	41	_____
d.	11	60	61	_____
e.	13	84	85	_____
f.	60	45	75	_____

2. Find the length of the line segment $\overline{AD}$ in each of these polygons.

a.

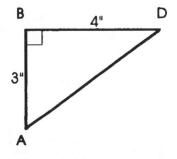

b.

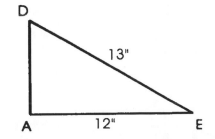

c.

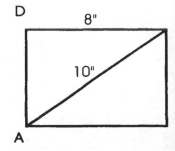

Fibonacci Numbers

Name_____

Leonardo Fibonacci was one of the most brilliant mathematicians of the Middle Ages. He discovered a sequence of numbers that is found in many areas of science. It is found in the leaf pattern of several plants, the arrangement of sections of a pineapple and bracts of a pine cone, as well as a way to describe the family tree of a male bee. Except for the first two terms, each term in the sequence is formed by adding the two preceding terms.

1. Add the missing terms to this sequence.

   1, 1, 2, 3, 5, 8, 13, 21, _____, _____, _____, _____, _____, _____, 610

2. Find the sum of the first five terms of this sequence. _____

3. How does this sum compare to the seventh term in the sequence? _____

   _____

4. Find the sum of the first eight terms of this sequence. _____

5. How does this compare to the tenth term of the sequence? _____

6. Without adding, what will be the sum of the first 10 terms? _____

   the first 13 terms? _____

Name _____

Here are some more interesting characteristics of Fibonacci numbers. Begin your investigation by writing the first 15 Fibonacci numbers in the sequence. Remember that the first two numbers are 1.

____ ____ ____ ____ ____

____ ____ ____ ____ ____

____ ____ ____ ____ ____

1. What do you notice about every fourth term in the sequence? _____

2. What do you notice about every fifth term of the sequence? _____

3. Find the squares of the first nine terms.

_____

4. Make a new sequence by adding each pair of consecutive squares (1 + 1, 2 + 3, etc.).

_____

5. What do you notice about this second sequence? _____

6. Find the sum of the squares (problem 3) and write the sum as a multiplication problem that follows the pattern that is shown below.

$1 + 1 = 2 = 1 \times 2$

$1 + 1 + 4 = 6 = 2 \times 3$

$1 + 1 + 4 + 9 = 15 = 3 \times 5$

$1 + 1 + 4 + 9 + 25 = 40 = $ _____ x _____

_____

_____

_____

Name_____

Use your knowledge of Fibonacci numbers to solve these problems.

1. Wild Willie and Dudley Dogood are playing poker. Willie starts the bidding with a certain bid. Dudley counters with a higher bid. Each bid after that is the sum of the two previous bids. Dudley ends the third round of bidding with a bid of $13.00. What were their first two bids?

2. George puts a certain sum of money (X) in the bank one week. The next week he deposits another amount of money (Y). The third week he deposits the sum of week 1 and week 2 deposits. Each week after that he deposits an amount equal to the two previous weeks' deposits. On the eighth week he deposits $34. What were his deposits for week 1 and week 2? How much money did he have in the bank at the end of eight weeks?

Name _____

Probability is a field of mathematics that was first formulated during the 1600s by a French philosopher named Blaise Pascal and has been used continually since by people in science and business. Many times in real life we do not know what the outcome of an event will be before it actually happens. Probability is a field of math that deals with predicting how likely it is that each possible outcome will happen. It is sometimes called *the mathematics of chance.*

Probability is applicable to many different activities in all areas of life where there are several possible outcomes. Some of these areas are:

- biology - hereditary characteristics
- politics - chances of winning
- meteorology - weather prediction
- insurance - life expectancy statistics
- manufacturing - quality control
- games of chance

One way to determine how likely it is that something will occur is to take a statistical approach. This means devising an experiment and repeating the experiment over and over again many times. If you repeat the experiment enough times, you will get results that are very close to the probability you can calculate mathematically. This is how insurance companies determine their life expectancy tables that let them predict how likely it is that any given person will die before a certain age.

Probability Experiment

If you flip a coin, there are only two outcomes, heads or tails, each of which should be equally likely. Flip a coin and keep track of the number of heads and tails:

	heads	tails
after 50 trials	_____	_____
after 100 trials	_____	_____
after 150 trials	_____	_____
after 200 trails	_____	_____

Did you get heads about as many times as you got tails? _____

Did the results get more accurate as you did more trials? _____

Name_____

When you use probability, you are usually looking at an event that has equally likely outcomes. One such event is flipping a coin. Providing it is a fair coin, there are two equally likely outcomes -- head or tail. The set of all possible outcomes is called the **sample space**. Each outcome in a sample space is called a **sample point**.

The sample space for tossing a coin is {H, T}. The sample points are H and T.

The sample space for tossing a penny and a dime would be S = {HH, HT, TH, TT}.

An **event** is a subset of the sample space. For the example above, you might be interested in the event of getting both heads or both tails. You could write this E = {HH, TT}

Match the sample spaces for the following events.

_____ 1. answers on a true-false question

_____ 2. rolling a six-sided die

_____ 3. days of the week

_____ 4. drawing one ball out of a bag that contains a red, blue, yellow, and green ball

_____ 5. drawing two balls out of a bag that contains a blue, yellow, and green ball

_____ 6. tossing a coin and rolling a die at the same time

_____ 7. sex of two children in a family

a. (by, bg, yg)

b. (BB, BG, GB, GG)

c. (r, b, y, g)

d. (T, F)

e. (Su, M, T, W, Th, F, Sa)

f. (H1, T1, H2, T2, H3, T3, H4, T4, H5, T5, H6, T6)

g. (1, 2, 3, 4, 5, 6)

8. What is the sample space for choosing a sock out of a drawer if there are two white socks, four black socks and two red socks?

_____

Name _____

Once you know the sample space for an event, it is easy to calculate the probability of any of the possible outcomes happening. The probability of an event happening is equal to the ratio of favorable outcomes to the total number of possible outcomes.

In the example of tossing a coin, there are two possible outcomes. If we want to know the probability of getting a head, there is only one chance of getting a head, so the probability would be 1 out of 2 or 1/2. We write it P(head) = 1/2

If you are choosing M & Ms out of a bag without looking and there are three yellows, three reds, three browns, the three oranges, there are four possible outcomes.
They are Y, R, B, and O. The probability for choosing any color would be:

P(Y) = 3/12 = 1/4
P(R) = 3/12 = 1/4
P(B) = 3/12 = 1/4
P(O) = 3/12 = 1/4

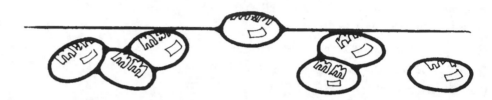

The rules for finding the probability of an event are:
- Probability of an event = $\dfrac{\text{favorable events}}{\text{total events}}$

- If an event has no chance of happening, it has a probability of 0.
- If an event is certain to happen, it has a probability of 1.
- The probability of an event is the sum of the probabilities of all the sample points it includes.

Example: P(orange or red M & M) = P(O) + P(R) = 1/4 + 1/4 = 1/2

---

1. If you are rolling a die, there are six equally-possible outcomes in the sample space. They are 1, 2, 3, 4, 5 and 6. What are the probabilities for the following events?

a. P(1) _____   f. P(2) _____

b. P(3) _____   g. P(4) _____

c. P(5) _____   h. P(6) _____

d. P(8) _____   i. P(number less than 10) _____

e. P(even) _____   j. P(odd) _____

Calculating Simple Probabilities

Name_____

1. Suppose you are throwing two dice. Complete this chart to show all the possible sample points and then find the probability of the following outcomes?

(1, 1)	(1, 2)	(1, 3)	(1, 4)	_____	_____
(2, 1)	(2,2)	(2, 3)	(2, 4)	_____	_____
(3, 1)	(3, 2)	(3, 3)	_____	_____	_____
_____	_____	_____	_____	(4, 5)	_____
_____	_____	_____	_____	_____	(5, 6)
_____	_____	_____	_____	_____	_____

a. P(sum is 6) = _____   b. P(sum is 3) =_____   c. P(sum is 15)_____

d. P(sum is 12) = _____   e. P(both even) = _____   f. P(one die is a 2) _____

2. Pretend you are throwing three different coins. Your sample space would look like this:

   HHH, HHT, HTH, HTT, THH, THT, TTH, TTT

   What are the probabilities for the following events?

   a. P(3 heads) = _____   d. P(3 tails) = _____

   b. P(2 heads) = _____   e. P(2 tails) = _____

   c. P(only 1 head) = _____   f. P(only 1 tail) = _____

Name _____

1. The following letters are lying face down on the Scrabble board. It is Josh's turn to draw a tile. What are the probabilities he will draw the following things?

    a. P(a vowel) _____   c. P(Z) = _____
    b. P(H) _____   d. P(a consonant) = _____

2. Tropical Treasures sells 10 gold fish for $1.00. In the tank they have 100 fish, all of which are gold except for twenty black fish. If the fish are scooped out randomly, what are the chances of getting a black fish?

3. You have four cards (red square, red triangle, blue square and blue diamond) that are face down on the table. If you randomly draw a card, what are the chances of drawing:

    a. blue diamond _____   d. blue _____

    b. square _____   e. red _____

    c. triangle _____   f. red diamond _____

Name_____

Here is the sample space for drawing a card from a deck of cards (no jokers). There are 52 possible outcomes. The probability of picking any sample point in this space is 1/52.

♣ A K Q J 10 9 8 7 6 5 4 3 2

♦ A K Q J 10 9 8 7 6 5 4 3 2

♥ A K Q J 10 9 8 7 6 5 4 3 2

♠ A K Q J 10 9 8 7 6 5 4 3 2

Here are some examples of probabilities for this sample space.

P(♥) = 13/52 = 1/4

P(8) = 4/52 = 1/13

P(A♣) = 1/52

P(8 or 9) = P(8) + P(9) = 4/52 + 4/52 = 8/52 = 2/13

Use this sample space to find the probabilities for the following events.

1. P(10♥) _____

2. P(black) _____

3. P(jack♦)_____

4. P(jack) _____

5. P(A, K, Q or J) _____

6. P(joker) _____

7. P(numbered card) _____

8. P(♣) _____

9. P(4) _____

10. P(11) _____

11. P(♥ or ♠) _____

12. P(♥ or ♦ or ♣ or ♠) _____

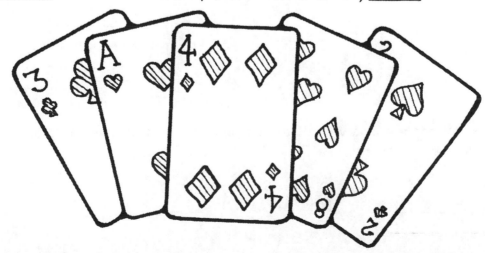

Name _____

You might have noticed in the exercises you have done so far that the sum of all the outcomes for an experiment is 1. For instance, the probability for each outcome for flipping two coins is 1/4. The sum of all possible outcomes is
P(HH) + P(TH) + P(HT) + P(TT) = 1/4 + 1/4 + 1/4 + 1/4 = 1

Suppose you are drawing a ball out of a box that has three black balls and 4 white balls. The sample space is

S = { B, B, B, W, W, W, W }

Since there are 4 white balls out of a total of 7 balls, the probability for the event of choosing a white ball is

P(white) = 4/7.

The elements of the sample set that are not elements in the event we are interested in are elements of the **complementary event**. In this case, the complement is the event "not white." We show this as P(not white) = 3/7

The probabilities that an event will happen and that it won't happen are called complementary events. The sum of the probabilities is 1.

P(happens) + P(doesn't happen) = 1

If you look at rolling a die, the probability of drawing a 4 is P(4) = 1/6 and P(not 4) = 5/6

P(4) + P(not 4) = 1/6 + 5/6 = 1

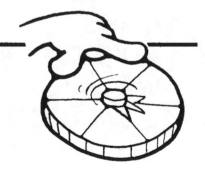

1. If you are spinning a spinner that has six numbered (1 - 6), equally-divided spaces, what is the probability for these complementary events?

    a. P(even) = _____   d. P(not even) = _____

    b. P(5 or greater) = _____   e. P(not greater than 5) = _____

    c. P(2) = _____   f. P(not 2) = _____

2. Consider the example above where you are flipping two coins. Write the probabilities for these complementary events.

    P(HH) = _____   P(not HH) = _____   P(HH) + P(not HH) = _____

    P(TH or HT) = _____   P(not TH or HT) = _____

Name _____

One way to list all the possible outcomes is to make a tree diagram. This techniques is especially useful if you have multiple events to keep track of. The diagram on the left below shows all the possible outcomes of throwing 3 coins. The diagram on the right shows all the possible outcomes for throwing 2 coins.

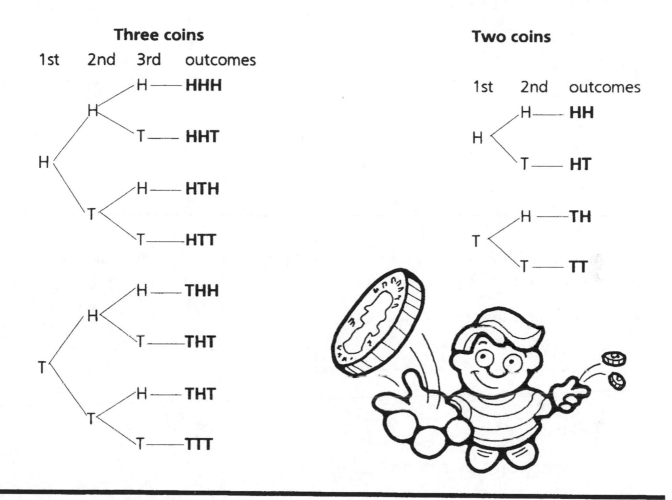

1. On another piece of paper make a tree diagram to show all the possible outcomes for the sex of two children in a family.

2. On another piece of paper make a tree diagram to show all the possible outcomes for drawing two balls out of a box of three balls colored red, white and blue. *(You will replace each ball before drawing the next one, so you will always have three balls from which to choose.)*

3. Use these tree diagrams to help you find the probability for each event listed below:

   a. both girls _____   d. two red balls _____

   b. a girl and a boy (either order)_____   e. 1 red, 1 white _____

   c. two boys_____   f. only 1 blue ball _____

Name_____

1. Make tree diagrams to show all the possible outcomes for each of these situations.

    a. Rolling two dice

    b. Choosing two marbles out of a jar that contains yellow, red, black and purple marbles (marbles are replaced after each draw)

2. How many possible outcomes are there for rolling two dice? _____ What are the probabilities for the following events?

    a. both dice show the same number _____

    b. sum of the dice is 7 _____

    c. sum of the dice is 2 _____

    d. sum of the dice is less than 5 _____

    e. sum of the dice is greater than 12 _____

3. How many possible outcomes are there for drawing two marbles from four different colors? _____ What are the probabilities for the following events?

    a. both marbles are purple _____

    b. the first marble drawn is red _____

    c. one marble is yellow and one is black _____

    d. both marbles are the same color _____

    e. the last marble drawn is black _____

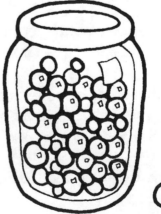

Name_____

When you are figuring the probability of several things happening in succession, one way you can do it is to make a tree diagram and use the list of outcomes to count the favorable events and figure the probability (lesson 9). Another way is to multiply the probabilities of each happening. This rule applies to events that are **independent**; that is, neither event depends on the other.

Multiplication Rule

If E and F are independent events, the probability of E then F is the product of the probability of the two events

P(E then F) = P(E) x P(F)

For example, if you are rolling a die twice and want to know the probability that you will roll two ones (1, 1), you would calculate the probability this way.

    P(1, 1) = P(1 on first roll then 1 on second roll)

    P(1) x P(1) = 1/6 x 1/6 = 1/36

Another example would be finding the probability that out of three children in a family, all three would be boys. The sex of each child in a family is an independent event, that is, having a boy for a first child does not affect the outcome of the second or third child, so you could use the multiplication method.

Each birth has two equally-likely outcomes (boy or girl), so P(boy) = P(girl) = 1/2.

To find the probability of getting three boys, you multiply the probabilities of each event:

    P(BBB) = P(B) x P(B) x P(B) = 1/2 x 1/2 x 1/2 = 1/8

---

1. Write a multiplication sentence to find the probabilities for the following events.

    a. having two boys in a two-child family_____

    b. rolling a 3 and then a 4 when rolling a die twice _____

    c. rolling an even then an odd number when a die is rolled twice _____

    d. getting an even number three times in a row on a spinner numbered 1 to 10_____

Name _____

Find the probabilities for the single events of rolling a die, flipping a coin, spinning a spinner and drawing cards from a deck of card.

1. Rolling dice

    a. P(6) _____

    b. P(even) _____

Flipping coins

    c. P(head) _____

    d. P(tail) _____

2. Spin a ten-section spinner

    a. P(3) _____

    b. P(even) _____

    c. P(7) _____

Draw cards from a deck

    d. P(♥) _____

    e. P(4) _____

    f. P(numbered card) _____

Use the probabilities you calculated above to determine the probability of these successive events.

Experiment	Desired outcome	Probability
3. flip coin and roll die	(head, 6)	_____
4. spin spinner and roll die	(7, 6)	_____
5. draw card, flip a coin	(numbered card, head)	_____
6. flip coin and spin spinner	(tail, even)	_____
7. spin spinner twice	(3, 7)	_____
8. draw card then spin spinner	(4, 3)	_____
9. draw card, put it back and draw again	(♥ , ♥)	_____

Name_____

As you learned in the last lesson, you can find the probability of successive events by multiplying the probabilities of each event. So far the events you have worked with are **independent events**. This means that the events have no influence on each other.

Dependent events are influenced by each other. An example would be drawing a card from a deck of playing cards and not replacing it before you drew the second card. The chances of getting any particular card on the first draw is 1 out of 52, but the chances of getting a particular card on the second draw is now 1 out of 51. You can still use the multiplication method, but you have to look carefully at the probabilities of each event, because the probabilities will change.

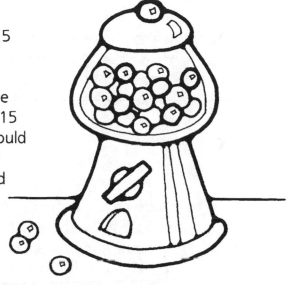

For example, a gumball machine has 20 white balls, 15 red balls, 10 yellow balls, 10 green balls, and 5 black balls, for a total of 60 balls. You want to get two gumballs and want them both to be red. The first time you put in your money, your chance of getting red is 15 out of 60. If you got a red ball the first time, there would only be 14 red balls and 59 balls total from which to choose, so the chance of getting a red ball the second time is 14/59.

The probability of two red gumballs is:

P(RR) = 15/60 x 14/59 = 210/3540 = 7/118

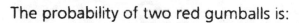

Find the probability of these successive happenings with dependent events.

Drawing cards out of a deck
(without replacement)

Drawing beans out of a jar that has
5 red beans, 10 black beans, and
15 green beans (without replacement)

1. P(1, 2 any suit) _____

6. P(R, B) _____

2. P(♥, ♥, ♥) _____

7. P(B, B) _____

3. P(♦, ♣) _____

8. P(G, G, G) _____

4. P(4, 4, 4) _____

9. P(R, B, R) _____

5. P(J, Q) _____

10. P(B, G, B) _____

Name _____

Find the probability of for the following events. Some of these represent independent events and some are dependent events.

1. Three friends, (Geno, Brice, Jamie, and Miguel) draw straws to see who will drive to the game each week. What is the probability that Brice will have to drive three weeks in a row?

2. Mrs. Diaz puts the names of all 30 students in a bowl and draws out a name each week. After the name is drawn, it is not returned to the bowl. The person whose name is drawn gets to choose the bonus spelling words for the week. What is the probability that Jill will be drawn the first week and her friend Carrie will be drawn the second week?

3. Rachel has a dozen eggs in the refrigerator, half of which are brown and half of which are white. Without looking she reaches in the refrigerator and gets two eggs for making cookies. What is the probability that both of the eggs are white?

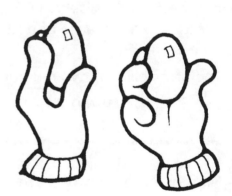

4. Sir Night is on his way to the castle to help a damsel in distress. He has two crossroads at which he has to make a decision about which road to take. What is the probability that he will reach the castle? What is the probability he will face a dragon?

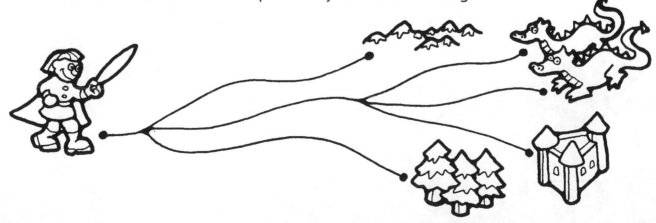

Name_____

1. If you draw two cards out of the deck of 52 cards (replacing the first card before you draw the second card), what are the probabilities for the following events?

a. P(♠, ♠) _____

b. P(♣, ♠) _____

c. P(2♥, 2♦) _____

d. P(8, 8) _____

e. P(both numbered cards) _____

f. P(both face cards *) _____

g. P(Q, K) _____

h. P(both kings) _____

Note: A face card is a king, queen or jack.

2. You spin a spinner that has ten equally divided spaces, numbered 1 through 10, half of which are green and half of which are pink. What are the probabilities for the following events?

a. P(10) _____

b. P(greater than 5) _____

c. P(11) _____

d. P(green) _____

e. P(less than 3) _____

f. P(not green) _____

3. You spin the spinner from the above problem twice. What are the chances your two spins will be:

a. P(1, 2) _____

b. P(both even) _____

c. P(sum = 5) _____

d. P(pink, pink) _____

e. P(pink, green) _____

f. P(sum = 1) _____

Name _____

While you have learned how to mathematically compute the probability that a given event will happen, sometimes you may wish to recreate the actual event or a simulation of the event. When you are trying to simulate an event to determine the likelihood of the occurrence, the greater the number of trials, the more accurate your results will be. You may not get a very accurate estimation if you perform the experiment only 10 times, but if you repeat it thousands of times, your results will approach the mathematical probability.

In some cases, it is hard to repeat your experiment over and over again, so you must find some other way to conduct the experiment. If you want to simulate determining whether a child will be a boy or a girl, you might toss a coin, as both events have a probability of 1/2. When insurance companies want to determine how likely it is that someone will die at a certain age, they compile statistics of thousands of people, their death age and health factors. From this, they determine the probability that someone will live to a certain age.

Guidelines for conducting a simulation to determine the probability of an event

1. Design an experiment that fits the problem
2. Determine what a trial represents
3. Describe a successful trial
4. Conduct a large number of trials and record the results
5. Compute the probability

Probability =   number of successful trials
                total number of trials

Use these guidelines to conduct an experiment for one of the following things:

a. chances that a rat in a cage will choose one of three doors if each door has a equal likelihood of being picked

b. chances that a bug will land on any one of the petals of an eight-petaled flower

c. chances that you can get a passing grade by guessing on a true-false test

d. chances that if you pick a word at random from the dictionary, it will have two-syllables

e. chances that if you asked everyone in the country their preference for car color, the favorite color would be blue

Answers

Magic Squares

Lesson 1 - page 6

```
4  9  2
3  5  7
8  1  6      sum = 15
```

Lesson 2 - page 7

```
8  1  6          4  9  2
3  5  7          3  5  7
4  9  2          8  1  6
```
answers will vary

Lesson 3 - page 8

Answers will vary. One correct arrangement is:

```
18  21   6      9  10   5       6  26  22
 3  15  27      4   8  12      34  18   2
24   9  12     11   6   7      14  10  30


 8  28  24     12  14   4
36  20   4      2  10  18
16  12  32     16   6   8
```

Lesson 4 - page 9

```
 7  12   1  14
 2  13   8  11
16   3  10   5
 9   6  15   4
```
Answers will vary for the second square

```
23   6  19   2  15
10  18   1  14  22
17   5  13  21   9
 4  12  25   8  16
11  24   7  20   3     sum = 65
```

Lesson 5 - page 10

Squares A, C, D are magic.
Squares B, E are not magic.

Lesson 6 - page 11

1. 4, 10, 16;   6, 10, 14;   8, 10, 12;   2, 10, 18
2. 6, 15, 24;   12, 15, 18;   3, 15, 27;   9, 15, 21
3. 9, 10, 11;   6, 10, 14;   7, 10, 13;   8, 10, 12

Lesson 7 - page 12

sum is 15

Lesson 8 - page 13

```
10  3  8          19  12  17
 5  7  9          14  16  18
 6  11  4         15  20  13
magic sum = 21    magic sum = 48

17  24   1   8  15
23   5   7  14  16
 4   6  13  20  22
10  12  19  21   3
11  18  25   2   9
magic sum = 65
```

Lesson 9 - page 14

magic sum = 34

Lesson 10 - page 15

```
19   5   6  16
 8  14  13  11
12  10   9  15
 7  17  18   4
magic sum = 46

80  10  15  65     25  11  12  22
25  55  50  40     14  20  19  17
45  35  30  60     18  16  15  21
20  70  75   5     13  23  24  10
magic sum = 170    magic sum = 70
```

Lesson 11 - page 16

1. circle 15 and 14 in bottom row
2. 34   3. 34
4. 19, 15   5. 21, 13
6. 34   7. 34

Lesson 12 - page 17

1. 260   2. 4 x 4
3. 130   4. 130
5. 130
6 a. 1, 2, 3, 4   b. 13, 14, 15, 16
  c. 49, 50, 51, 52   d. 61, 62, 63, 64

Lesson 13 - page 18

```
1.  9   2   7      2.  26  24  34
    4   6   8          36  28  20
    5  10   3          22  32  30
    sum = 18           sum = 84

3.  40  15  20     4.  67   1  43
     5  25  45         13  37  61
    30  35  10         31  73   7
    sum = 75           sum = 111

5.  14  10  30     6.  45  63   9
    34  18   2          3  39  75
     6  26  22         69  15  33
    sum = 54           sum = 117
```

Lesson 14 - page 19

```
16   3  10   5        23  12   1  20   9
 1  12   7  14         4  18   7  21  15
 8  13   2  11        10  24  13   2  16
 9   6  15   4        11   5  19   8  22
                      17   6  25  14   3
1. sum = 34           3. sum = 65

 8   5.5   2   3.5     8    1   11/2  61/2
2.5   3   8.5   5     21/2  51/2  5    4
7.5   6   1.5   4     41/2  31/2  3    6
 1   4.5   7   6.5     2    7    71/2  1/2
2. sum = 19           4. sum = 17
```

Lesson 15 - page 20
1. 65   2. 39
3. 123   4. 205   5. 287

Topology

Lesson 1 - page 21
5, 7, C, G, I, J

Lesson 2 - page 22
1. E   4. A
2. C   5. B
3. D

Lesson 3 - page 23
a. 1   b. 2   c. 1
d. =   e. 2   f. =

Lesson 4 - page 24
1 - bat, pyramid, coin
2 - wreath, nut, key, ring
3 - note book paper, pretzel, vest

Lesson 5 - page 25
a, e, f are simple closed curves

Lesson 6 - page 26
inside - C, D, E, G
outside - A, B, F, H

Lesson 7 - page 27
4. impossible   5 and 6. both drawing are possible

Lesson 8 - page 28

	R	V	A
1.	3	4	5
2.	3	3	4
3.	5	5	8
4.	3	6	7
5.	5	3	6
6.	5	7	10

7. yes

Lesson 9 - page 29
1. C   2. NT   3. C   4. O

Lesson 10 - page 30
1. a. even   b. odd   c. even   d. odd
   m. even   n. even   o. odd   p. odd
2. a. Open   b. Open   c. Closed
3. not traceable

Lesson 12 - page 32
0, 1, and 2 twists - two sided; ½ and 1½ and are one-sided

Lesson 13 - page 33
1 twist - 1/2 cut yields one long loop; 1/3 and 1/4 cuts
   yield two interlocked loops (one small and one long)
2 twists - both cuts yield two interlocked loops, different
   widths but same length
3 twists - 1/2 cut yields 1 loop; 1/3 and 1/4 cuts yield
   two interlocked loops of different size
Answers will vary.

Lesson 14 - page 34
1. a. 3   b. 2   c. 3
   d. 2   e. 2   f. 4
2. answers will vary

Number Characteristics

Lesson 1 - page 35
1. add 2, add 3, add 4, add 5, add 6, etc.
2. a. add 2   b. add 3
   c. multiply by 2   d. square each whole number
   e. multiples of 10   f. divide by 2

Lesson 2 - page 36
9 - 45   10 - 55   11 - 66   12 - 78
13 - 91   14 - 105

Lesson 3 - page 37
1. $25 = 5 \times 5$ $36 = 6 \times 6$ $49 = 7 \times 7$
   $64 = 8 \times 8$ $81 = 9 \times 9$ $100 = 10 \times 10$
2. $n \times n$
3. $9 = 1 + 3 + 5$ $16 = 1 + 3 + 5 + 7$
   $25 = 1 + 3 + 5 + 7 + 9$ $36 = 1 + 3 + 5 + 7 + 9 + 11$
   $49 = 1 + 3 + 5 + 7 + 9 + 11 + 13$
   $64 = 1 + 3 + 5 + 7 + 9 + 11 + 13 + 15$
   $81 = 1 + 3 + 5 + 7 + 9 + 11 + 13 + 15 + 17$

Lesson 4 - page 38

1.			2.	
1	1			
3	4			
6	9			
10	16		$16 = 10 + 6$	
15	25		$25 = 15 + 10$	
21	36		$36 = 21 + 15$	
28	49		$49 = 28 + 21$	
36	64		$64 = 36 + 28$	
45	81		$81 = 45 + 36$	
55	100			

Lesson 5 - page 39
1. $30 = 5 \times 6$ $42 = 6 \times 7$
   $56 = 7 \times 8$ $72 = 8 \times 9$
2. $20 = 2 + 4 + 6 + 8$ $30 = 2 + 4 + 6 + 8 + 10$
   $42 = 2 + 4 + 6 + 8 + 10 + 12$
   $56 = 2 + 4 + 6 + 8 + 10 + 12 + 14$
   $72 = 2 + 4 + 6 + 8 + 10 + 12 + 14 + 16$
   $90 = 2 + 4 + 6 + 8 + 10 + 12 + 14 + 16 + 18$

3.			
2	1	42	21
6	3	56	28
12	6	72	36
20	10	90	45
30	15	110	55

Lesson 6 - page 40
1. prime numbers are 2, 3, 5, 7, 11, 13, 17, 19, 23, 29,
   31, 37, 41, 43, 47, 53, 59, 61, 67, 71, 73, 79, 83, 89,
   97
2. (11, 13) (17, 19) (29, 31) (41, 43) (59, 61) (71, 73)

Lesson 7 - page 41
Several answers are possible; here are 2 for each number:
$16 = 11 + 5; 13 + 3$ $18 = 13 + 5; 11 + 7$
$20 = 17 + 3; 13 + 7$ $22 = 19 + 3; 17 + 5$

28 = 23 + 5; 17 + 11   34 = 29 + 5; 31 + 3
46 = 41 + 5; 17 + 29   52 = 47 + 5; 41 + 11
68 = 61 + 7; 31 + 37   70 = 67 + 3; 29 + 41
88 = 83 + 5; 29 + 59   96 = 89 + 7; 59 + 37
100 = 97 + 3; 71 + 29   106 = 17 + 89; 53 + 53

Lesson 8 - page 42
1. 59 pieces   2. 493 (29 x 17)   3. 15

Lesson 9 - page 43
answers will vary

Lesson 10 - page 44
1. a. 25 + 144 = 169   b. 49 + 576 = 625
   c. 81 + 1600 = 1681   d. 121 + 3600 = 3721
   e. 169 + 7056 = 7225   f. 3600 + 2025 = 5625
2. a. 5"   b. 5"   c. 6"

Lesson 11 - page 45
1. 34, 55, 89, 144, 233, 377, 610
2. 12   3. 1 less than 7th term
4. 54   5. 1 less than 8th term
6. 10 term = 143; 13 terms = 609

Lesson 12 - page 46
1. multiple of 3   2. multiple of 5
3. 1, 1, 4, 9, 25, 64, 169, 441, 1156
4. 2, 5, 13, 34, 89, 233, 610, 1597
5. every other Fibonacci number
6. 40 = 5 x 8
   1 + 1 + 4 + 9 + 25 + 64 = 104 = 8 x 13
   1 + 1 + 4 + 9 + 25 + 64 + 169 = 273 = 13 x 21
   1 + 1 + 4 + 9 + 25 + 64 + 169 + 441 = 714 = 21 x 34

Lesson 13 - page 47
1. Dudley $1; Willie $2   2. 1 - $1; 2 - $2; total - $87

Probability

Lesson 1 - page 48
Answers will vary.

Lesson 2 - page 49
1. d   2. g   3. e   4. c
   5. a   6. f   7. b
2. (W, W, B, B, B, B, R, R)

Lesson 3 - page 50
1. a. 1/6   b. 1/6   c. 1/6
   d. 0   e. 3/6   f. 1/6
   g. 1/6   h. 1/6   i. 1   j. 1/2

Lesson 4 - page 51
1. a. 5/36   b. 2/36   c. 0
   d. 1/36   e. 9/36   f. 11/36
2. a. 1/8   d. 1/8
   b. 3/8   e. 3/8
   c. 3/8   f. 3/8

Lesson 5 - page 52
1. a. 2/7   b. 2/7   c. 1/7   d. 5/7
2. 20/100 = 2/10
3. a. 1/4   d. 2/4
   b. 2/4   e. 2/4
   c. 1/4   f. 0

Lesson 6 - page 53
1. 1/52   7. 36/52
2. 1/2   8. 13/52 = 1/4
3. 1/52   9. 4/52 = 1/13
4. 4/52 = 1/13   10. 4/52 = 1/13
5. 16/52   11. 26/52 = 1/2
6. 0   12. 1

Lesson 7 - page 54
1. a. 3/6 = 1/2   d. 3/6 = 1/2
   b. 2/6   c. 4/6
   c. 1/6   f. 5/6
2. 1/4   3/4   1
   2/4   2/4

Lesson 8 - Page 55
1. Outcomes are GG, GB, BB, BG
2. Outcomes are RR, RW, RB, BR, BW, BB, WR, WW, WB
3. a. 1/4   d. 1/9
   b. 2/4   e. 2/9
   c. 1/4   f. 4/9

Lesson 9 - page 56
2. 36 outcomes a. 6/36   b. 6/36
   c. 1/36   d. 6/36   e. 0
3. 16 outcomes a. 1/16   b. 4/16
   c. 2/16   d. 4/16   e. 4/16

Lesson 10 - page 57
1. a. 1/2 x 1/2 = 1/4   b. 1/6 x 1/6 = 1/36
c. 1/2 x 1/2 = 1/4   d. 1/2 x 1/2 x 1/2 = 1/8

Lesson 11 - page 58
1. a. 1/6   c. 1/2
   b. 1/2   d. 1/2
2.. a. 1/10   d. 1/4
   b. 1/2   e. 1/13
   c. 1/10   f. 36/52 = 9/13
3. 1/12   4. 1/60   5. 9/26
6. 1/4   7. 1/100   8. 1/130   9. 1/16

Lesson 12 - page 59
1. 4/663   6. 10/174 = 5/87
2. 11/850   7. 3/29
3. 13/204   8. 13/116
4. 1/5525   9. 5/609
5. 4/663   10. 45/812

Lesson 13 - page 60
1. 1/64   2. 1/870
3. 5/22   4. castle - 1/9; dragon 2/9

Lesson 14 - page 61
1. a. 1/16   b. 1/16
   c. 1/2704   d. 1/169
   e. 81/169   f. 9/169
   g. 1/169   h. 1/169
2. a. 1/10   b. 1/2   c. 0
   d. 1/2   e. 1/5   f. 1/2
3. a.1/100   b. 1/4   c. 1/25
   d. 1/4   e. 1/4   f. 0

Printed in the United States
by Baker & Taylor Publisher Services